• PEOPLES of NORTH AMERICA •

Sioux

VALERIE BODDEN

CREATIVE EDUCATION • CREATIVE PAPERBACKS

Published by Creative Education and Creative Paperbacks
P.O. Box 227, Mankato, Minnesota 56002
Creative Education and Creative Paperbacks
are imprints of The Creative Company
www.thecreativecompany.us

Design and production by Christine Vanderbeek
Art direction by Rita Marshall
Printed in the United States of America

Photographs by Alamy (Danita Delimont, GL Archive, INTERFOTO, North Wind Picture
Archives, Photos 12, allen russell, United Archives GmbH), Corbis (AP, GARY CAMERON/
Reuters, Corbis, Orjan F. Ellingvag, W. Langdon Kihn/National Geographic Society, Francis G.
Mayer, Richard Hewitt Stewart/National Geographic Society, Tarker, Marilyn Angel Wynn/
Nativestock Pictures), Dreamstime (Ken Backer), Getty Images (Chris Frank), iStockphoto
(chpaquette, ericfoltz, foofie), Shutterstock (Stefan Petru Andronache, Jill Battaglia,
branislavpudar, OHishiapply, Menno Schaefer, Transia Design, tur'tix), SuperStock (Christie's
Images Ltd.), Wikimedia Creative Commons (John C. H. Grabill Collection/Library of Congress)

Library of Congress Cataloging-in-Publication Data
Bodden, Valerie.
Sioux / Valerie Bodden.
p. cm. — (Peoples of North America) • Includes bibliographical references and index.
Summary: A history of the people and events that influenced the North American Indian
tribe known as the Sioux or Dakota, including warrior Crazy Horse and conflicts such as
the U.S.-Dakota War.
ISBN 978-1-60818-555-9 (hardcover)
ISBN 978-1-62832-156-2 (pbk)
1. Dakota Indians—History—Juvenile literature.
2. Dakota Indians—Social life and customs—Juvenile literature. I. Title.

E99.D1B715 2015
978.004'975243—dc23   2014041751

CCSS: RI.5.1, 2, 3, 5, 6, 8, 9; RH.6-8.4, 5, 6, 7, 8, 9

HC 9 8 7 6 5 4 3 2
PBK 9 8 7 6 5 4 3 2

PEOPLES *of* NORTH AMERICA

Sioux

VALERIE BODDEN

CREATIVE EDUCATION   •   CREATIVE PAPERBACKS

Table of Contents

◆━━ Sioux chiefs gathered together in 1899 (on ━━◆
page 3); a traditional Plains Indian tepee in
Colorado (pictured here)

Introduction

The people we know today as the Sioux once galloped horses over the vast expanse of North America's Great Plains. Winds bowed head-high grasses in the eastern part of this region, while farther west, the short grasses crunched underfoot. The fragrant scent of sage drifted through the air. Aside from the cottonwood trees that grew along the banks of the region's wide, shallow rivers, the landscape was unbroken. But it wasn't empty. Elk, pronghorn, deer, bears, coyotes, rabbits, and prairie dogs made their homes here. The Plains' most distinctive animal was the bison (commonly known as "buffalo" in the past). Huge herds tramped through the grasses, filling the landscape to the horizon. In many ways, the bison defined the Sioux lifestyle, as the Indians traveled the Plains in pursuit of these mighty animals.

The name "Sioux" comes from a French interpretation of an Ojibwa word meaning "little snakes." But the Sioux did not call themselves by this name. Instead, they referred to themselves as Dakota, Nakota (Yankton), or Lakota, depending on the band to which they belonged. These names meant "friends" or "allies." Although they lived in separate bands, the Sioux shared a common culture and religion. When their way of life was threatened by settlers in the 1800s, the Sioux resisted. Eventually, though, they were resettled on reservations. There they struggled to hold on to their old ways while adapting to a new life. Today, their traditional culture remains a vital part of life for many Sioux people, whether they live on the reservation or off.

SOUTH DAKOTA'S CUSTER STATE PARK IS
HOME TO APPROXIMATELY 1,300 BISON.

· SIOUX ·

From Woodlands to the Plains

PEOPLES of NORTH AMERICA

Although today we think of the Sioux as the great warriors of the Plains, they did not actually move onto the Great Plains until the late 1600s and early 1700s. Scholars disagree over where the earliest Sioux ancestors came from. Some say they migrated from the far north, near the Arctic Circle. Others contend that the Sioux originated in the southeastern part of North America. Most scholars agree, however, that by about A.D. 800, the ancestors of the Sioux had moved into the woodlands of what are today the states of Wisconsin and Minnesota. These Sioux ancestors may have lived in small family groups for a time before settling in larger, permanent villages around 1300. There they likely lived in bark lodges and hunted deer, rabbits, and other small game; harvested wild rice; and planted small gardens. A couple times a year, they may have sent hunting parties west to hunt bison on the Plains.

By the mid-1600s, the Sioux had split into three groups, each speaking a different **DIALECT** of the Siouan language and living in a different territory. The Dakota Sioux (also called the Santee) made up the easternmost group, near the Great Lakes. They spoke the Dakota dialect. To the southwest of the Dakota were the Yankton, who spoke the Nakota dialect. The Lakota

SIOUX LEADERS SUCH AS RED TOMAHAWK FOUGHT TO PROTECT THEIR ANCESTRAL HOMELAND BEFORE FINALLY MAKING PEACE.

By the late 1800s, the presence of American forts near Sioux camps helped restrict people's travels.

Sioux (also called Teton) lived farthest west, near the border of present-day Minnesota and South Dakota, and spoke Lakota. Each group was further divided into smaller bands. The Dakota, for example, were made up of the Mdewakanton, Wahpekute, Sisseton, and Wahpeton. The Yankton consisted of the Yankton and Yanktonai. And the Lakota were divided into seven bands: Oglala, Sicangu, Sihasapa, Miniconjou, Sans Arc, Oohenupa, and Hunkpapa. Individuals did not have to remain with the Sioux band they were born into, and they might travel from group to group frequently. The languages they spoke were all close enough to be mutually understood.

The Sioux were not the only American Indians in the area, though. The powerful Ojibwa (also called Ojibway, Ojibwe, or Chippewa) moved into the Great Lakes region as European settlers pushed west in the 1600s. The Ojibwa wanted the land to themselves, and they had acquired new weapons—guns—from French traders that proved useful in pushing the Sioux off their traditional lands and toward the Great Plains. According to 20th-century Sioux **MEDICINE MAN** Leonard Crow Dog, "We came from the land of the Great Lakes…. Then the French gave guns, matchlocks, to the Ojibway. We had only bows and arrows. So we were pushed toward the west." The Sioux may have also been lured toward the Plains by the promise of more plentiful game for both trade and food.

The Sioux move west likely began in the late 1600s and continued into the 1700s. The Dakota Sioux moved into southern and western Minnesota, while the Yankton moved into the eastern

⇒⇒ **ONE BISON, 200 USES** ⇐⇐ *The Sioux used every part of the bison to make nearly 200 different items. The hides were used as robes, while tanned skins were used for tepee covers and clothing. For thread, the Sioux used* **SINEW** *from the bison's back and legs. Horns were fashioned into spoons or bowls. Hooves were boiled to make glue, and bones were made into tools. The tail was used to swat flies. Even the stomach was used as a kettle. The skull served as an* **ALTAR** *for rituals.*

Dakotas. The Lakota spread past the Missouri River in the cen-
tral Dakotas, and their territory eventually encompassed parts
of present-day North and South Dakota, Montana, Nebraska,
Colorado, and Wyoming.

The move onto the Plains completely changed the Sioux way
of life, especially for the Lakota, who gave up their settled villages to become **NOMADIC**. They wandered across the Plains, fol-
lowing the bison herds they now relied on for food. The Dakota
and Yankton, on the other hand, maintained a settled lifestyle for
much of the year, traveling only at certain times to hunt.

On the Plains, most Sioux lived in tents called tepees. Tepees
were especially well suited for a mobile lifestyle, since they could
be set up and taken down quickly. At first, tepees had to be small,
because they were moved from camp to camp on **TRAVOIS** pulled
by dogs. Most tepees were only about 10 feet (3 m) across at the
base. This gave an entire Sioux family of 5 to 8 people a living
area of 80 square feet (7.4 sq m)—smaller than the average bed-
room in an American house today.

By the mid-1700s, the Sioux had acquired horses, which they
called *shunka wakan*, or "sacred dog." Horses allowed the Sioux

⇢⊶ **PIPES AND PRAYERS** ⊶⇠ *The Sioux believed that, long ago, the White Buffalo Woman—a woman who turned into a white bison calf—brought their people the sacred pipe. She told them to use the pipe, which had a long, decorated stem, in their rituals. The Sioux passed around the pipe at council meetings and conferences. They smoked it before vision quests and in sweat lodge ceremonies. For the Sioux, the smoke coming out of the pipe symbolized their prayers.*

to travel and hunt more efficiently, and they could also pull larger loads than dogs. Tepees became larger, expanding to about 15 feet (4.6 m) across. This more than doubled the interior living area. Tepees were made of 11 to 13 long, slender poles arranged into a cone shape and covered by 12 to 20 bison hides. During the summer, the bottoms of the hides could be rolled up to let the breeze pass through. In the winter, soil and rocks could be piled against the sides of the tepee to create a layer of insulation. The Sioux liked to say, "A beautiful tepee is like a good mother. She hugs her children to her and protects them from heat and cold, storm and rain."

The Sioux loved the Plains. Not only did the region provide them with bison and other foods such as currants, chokecherries, and prairie turnips, but it was also considered sacred. "We did not think of the great open plains, the beautiful rolling hills, and winding streams with tangled growth as 'wild,'" said 20th-century Oglala Sioux chief Luther Standing Bear. "To us, it was tame. Earth was bountiful, and we were surrounded with the blessings of the Great Mystery" (a figure whom the Sioux believed was the creator of the universe).

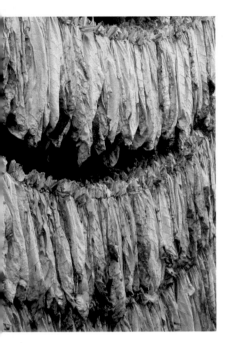

NOT A PROMINENT CROP IN THE PLAINS, TOBACCO BECAME VALUABLE FOR TRADE AS THE SIOUX RANGED FARTHER AFIELD.

The Sioux thought the Black Hills region of southwestern South Dakota was especially sacred. They called this low mountain range *Paha Sapa* and believed it to be "the heart of everything that is." According to Sioux legend, their people had originated under the earth of these tree-covered mountains. Every year, they gathered near the Black Hills to hold religious celebrations.

The Sioux were not the only American Indians to call the Great Plains home. But by the mid-1700s, the Lakota was one of the dominant tribes on the Plains. As they moved westward, they often pushed other tribes (such as the Crow, Cheyenne, Iowa, Ponca, Pawnee, Arikara, Mandan, Hidatsa, Assiniboine, and Kiowa) off their lands. Some of these tribes, such as the Crow, Pawnee, and Assiniboine, became longtime Sioux enemies. But the Sioux later formed an alliance with the Cheyenne. They traded with many Plains tribes as well. From the agricultural Hidatsa and Mandan, they received squash, corn, beans, and tobacco in return for shirts, leggings, and bison-skin robes. American Indians with ties to European traders provided the Sioux with knives, guns, and other European goods as well.

The tribes that lived on the Plains spoke many different languages. So they developed a unique sign language to communicate. Among the peoples to use the Plains sign language were the Sioux, Pawnee, Shoshone, Arapaho, Cheyenne, Crow, Kiowa, Blackfeet, and Nez Perce. At times, people even used signs when talking to others of their own tribe to enhance the meaning of what they said, especially when telling a story.

· SIOUX ·
Home on the Plains
PEOPLES of NORTH AMERICA

For much of the year, the larger Sioux bands on the Plains broke up into smaller groups known as *tiyospaye*, or camps. Each tiyospaye generally consisted of 10 or more families, who were often related to one another. The families of a tiyospaye lived and hunted together as they moved across the grasslands after the bison.

Each tiyospaye was led by a headman, or chief. Although the headman was the acknowledged leader of the tiyospaye, he did not have absolute authority. If the people did not like what the headman had to say, they could ignore him, replace him, or leave to form a new tiyospaye. According to the Oglala Sioux named Bad Bear, "If [the headman] was wise and the people found that his advice was good, then they obeyed him…. If a chief were brave and a warrior, then his camp would be large. If he were a coward, then his people would leave him."

Life on the Plains changed along with the seasons. Hunting began in the spring as the tiyospaye followed the bison. They might stay in each campsite for a few days or a few weeks. When the herds moved on, the tiyospaye followed. They generally traveled 10 to 15 miles (16.1–24.1 km) before setting up a new camp. Then the hunt began again. Sometimes each man hunted alone,

FAMILIES WITHIN A SIOUX TIYOSPAYE COOPER-
ATED WITH ONE ANOTHER AND WORKED TO LIVE
IN HARMONY.

BISON HUNTERS
HAD TO GET AS
CLOSE AS THEY
COULD TO FATALLY
SHOOT OR SPEAR
THE ENORMOUS
CREATURES.

tracking a bison and then killing it with a bow and arrow or a lance. Often, though, small groups of men from the tiyospaye joined forces to pursue the bison.

The largest bison hunts were held in the summer, when the various tiyospaye gathered for tribal hunts. Mounted on horses, the men joined forces to pursue the bison. Luther Standing Bear described how it felt to participate in such a hunt: "All I could hear was the roar and rattle of the hoofs of the buffalo as they thundered along…. I knew if my pony went down and one of those big animals stepped on me, it would be my last day on Earth…. I rode right up alongside the buffalo…. Drawing an arrow from my quiver, and holding to my pony with all the strength of my legs, I fitted the arrow and let drive with all my strength."

In addition to large hunts, tribal celebrations were also held in the summer. These celebrations were a time for games, horse races, feasts, and religious ceremonies. After the summer celebrations, the tribes again broke up, and each tiyospaye went its own way. The men continued to hunt, while the women dried meat and fruit to stock up on food for winter.

By the time the snow fell, the tiyospaye had settled into their winter camps. These were generally made in sheltered areas along rivers or near the Black Hills. The people passed the long winter months in their tepees, listening as the old men told the stories their people had been telling for generations.

In the wintertime, war and raiding parties rode out from the camp infrequently. But during the rest of the year, raiding

⇒⊸ **BRAVE AS A KIT FOX** ⊸⇐ *Many Sioux warriors joined military societies, such as the Badgers, Brave Hearts, or Plain Lance Owners. Among the bravest warriors were the members of the Kit Fox society. They each wore a long sash across their middle, and when they reached the battlefield, they staked the trailing end of the sash to the ground. They remained staked to that spot until they defeated their enemy, were killed, or were freed by a fellow warrior. Their leaders had to vow never to retreat from battle.*

parties often tore into the camps of other Plains tribes. Most battles involved surprise attacks carried out by a small war party. For the Sioux, war was primarily a way for a young warrior to prove his bravery through acts known as "counting coup." This meant getting close enough to touch an enemy—with one's hand, a weapon, or a "coup stick"—and then escape alive. Another way to count coup was to steal an enemy's horses. In addition to wars to earn coup, the Sioux fought ongoing battles with neighboring peoples, such as the Pawnee, over hunting grounds. Such battles often became bloody.

While men had responsibility for hunting and making war, women took care of the family's shelter, food, and clothing needs. The tepee and everything in it belonged to the wife, and she was responsible for setting it up and taking it down every time the camp moved. Women also prepared the bison and other animals the men brought home from the hunt. They dried the meat and readied the hides, bones, and horns to be used for clothing and tools. In addition, women made the family's clothing, medicine pouches, and knife sheaths from deer, elk, or bison hides and skins. Instead of pottery, which certainly would have broken during the tiyospaye's many moves, women made parfleches. These rawhide containers were used to hold food, tools, and other supplies. To decorate them, the women created elaborate patterns using dyed porcupine quills.

Sioux men were allowed to marry more than one woman, and in many cases, they took their wife's younger sister as a second wife. The wives divided the work of the household between them. Taking more than one wife also allowed a man to have more children. The Sioux looked upon their children as their greatest gift. Although children were rarely disciplined, they were not allowed to cry. This way they learned to remain silent

THE TRADITIONAL LAKOTA BELIEF THAT A CHILD CHOSE HIS OR HER PARENTS IMPARTED A SENSE OF EACH BABY'S BEING A GIFT.

when on the hunt or hiding from enemies. A child was given a name shortly after birth but might later be given a different name to reflect personality traits or great deeds. A boy might receive a new name after experiencing his first bison hunt or vision quest, for example.

The vision quest was a Sioux tradition for all young men. A boy's first vision quest usually took place when he was a teen. First, he would enter the sweat lodge, a structure made of bent willow branches and bison hides and filled with hot steam. Then he would be taken into the wilderness, where he remained, alone, for four days. Afterward, a medicine man helped him interpret whatever vision he had had, which was meant to guide his life. Although a boy's first vision quest marked an important step on his journey to manhood, both men and women made numerous vision quests throughout their lives.

The vision quest was one of the many important spiritual ceremonies carried out by the Sioux. The Sioux believed that

⤛═ **MAN VS. EAGLE** ═⤜ *Sioux warriors who had counted coup earned golden eagle feathers. But they had to catch and kill the eagles themselves. To do this, a warrior dug a three-foot-deep (0.9 m) pit and covered it with sticks, dirt, grass, and bait, such as a dead jackrabbit. The warrior waited inside the pit, and when an eagle landed on the roof, he pulled it into the pit and killed it with his bare hands. He wore the feathers in his hair, and when he had earned enough, he fashioned them into a headdress.*

Wakan Tanka, or the Great Mystery, created and existed in every element of the universe. "Every object in the world has a spirit, and that spirit is *wakan*. Thus the spirit of the tree or things of that kind … are also wakan," the Lakota Sioux medicine man Sword explained. Among all the objects in the universe, the Sioux believed the sun, sky, and earth were especially sacred. The bison was revered as well.

The most important religious ceremony was the Sun Dance, which was celebrated every year during the summer tribal gathering. For the Sun Dance, warriors who had **FASTED** danced around a sacred pole. In the Lakota tradition, the warriors were attached to the pole by skewers on the end of rawhide ropes. The skewers were thrust into the warriors' chests or backs. As the warriors danced, the skewers ripped at their skin, showing their humility before the Great Spirit and serving as a sacrifice to earn the Spirit's protection over the entire tribe.

THE LARGEST BIRDS OF PREY IN NORTH AMERICA, GOLDEN EAGLES HAVE WING-SPANS OF 6 TO 7.5 FEET (1.8–2.3 M).

SIOUX

Early Encounters

PEOPLES *of* NORTH AMERICA

The first European explorers had established colonies in North America in the 1500s. But the Sioux were among the last tribes to encounter these newcomers. The first recorded contact with any Europeans occurred when a French expedition came upon the Sioux in the woodlands of Wisconsin and Minnesota in 1659.

Although their early contact with Europeans was infrequent, the Sioux obtained European goods from other Indian tribes. In exchange for furs, the Sioux could get horses, axes, knives, blankets, cloth, and other items. By the mid-1700s, the Sioux were dealing directly with French and British traders who had moved to the Great Plains. In general, the Sioux had good relationships with these early traders, many of whom adopted the lifestyle of the Plains. Some even married Sioux women or became "adopted" members of Sioux families.

In the early 1800s, trade on the Plains increased as American traders joined the British and French. The Sioux traded horses, hides, and meat in return for coffee, sugar, glass beads, and guns. Although many of the goods made the daily life of the Sioux easier, not all trades had a positive impact. Among the things traders brought to the Plains was whiskey. With the introduction

FUR TRADERS ON THE MISSOURI RIVER CAME ACROSS VARIOUS SIOUX CAMPS IN THE DAKOTAS, NEBRASKA, AND IOWA.

of alcohol and the effects its uncontrolled usage had on them, the Sioux suddenly found themselves dealing with crimes such as theft, assault, and murder.

Traders also brought diseases such as smallpox and **CHOLERA** to the region. Indians had no natural defenses against these diseases, so their bodies were not able to fight the infections' spread. Because the Sioux lived in small groups that traveled frequently, they were not as affected by these diseases as other tribes. Even so, many Sioux were killed in a smallpox and cholera outbreak in the early 1800s.

By 1820, the Sioux were growing alarmed by the number of settlers entering their territories. That year, a Sioux medicine man drew a **PICTOGRAPH** of one of the year's major events. Translated, it meant, "A white man built his house on Sioux lands without permission." In 1837, the Dakota Sioux were pressured to sell their lands east of the Mississippi River to the U.S. government. They gave up more land in 1851 and were resettled on a small reservation in Minnesota.

Meanwhile, on the Plains, the wagon trains passing through Sioux territory seemed to get longer every day. By the 1840s, the Sioux had had enough. They began to send out raiding parties to attack the wagons. The U.S. Army moved into the area to protect the Americans and often exchanged gunfire with the Sioux.

In September 1851, the U.S. government called for a peace conference at Fort Laramie in present-day Wyoming. Ten thousand Indians from 13 tribes attended the conference, where they signed the Treaty of Fort Laramie (1851). It assigned specific boundaries to each tribe and required them to maintain peace with one another and with settlers passing through on the **OREGON TRAIL** and other routes west. It also allowed the U.S. to build roads and

PICTOGRAPHS ON THE LONE DOG WINTER COUNT RECORD 70 YEARS' WORTH OF EVENTS IN A YANKTONAI COMMUNITY.

TEACHING WHITE WAYS *In the late 1800s and early 1900s, many Sioux families sent their children to boarding schools such as the Carlisle Indian Industrial School in Pennsylvania. Students were forced to wear American-style clothing. Boys had their hair cut short. Any student caught speaking his or her native language was physically punished. "The change in clothing, housing, food, and confinement combined with lonesomeness was too much, and in three years, nearly one half of the children from the Plains were dead," Luther Standing Bear later said of the school.*

forts throughout the region. In return for all these concessions, the government pledged to provide the Sioux with food, livestock, and money.

The peace did not last long. In 1854, a Lakota warrior killed a lame cow that had wandered off from a settler's wagon. In response, U.S. Army Lieutenant John Grattan marched with a group of about 30 soldiers into the Sioux camp (which contained some 1,200 warriors). He demanded that Chief Conquering Bear turn over the warrior for arrest. Conquering Bear refused, instead offering horses as payment for the dead cow. Looking for an excuse to fight, Grattan ordered his soldiers to open fire, and Conquering Bear was killed. The Sioux retaliated, killing Grattan and all his men in what became known as the Grattan Fight.

The Grattan Fight marked the start of the Sioux Wars, which would continue for more than 30 years. Most battles of the Sioux Wars were skirmishes between small groups of Sioux warriors and U.S. soldiers. But some, such as the Sioux Uprising of 1862 (also known as the U.S.-Dakota War), were bigger. When the Dakota Sioux had given up their land in 1851 and moved onto reservations in Minnesota, the government had promised to

⟹ GIVING IT ALL AWAY ⟸ *Generosity was highly valued among the Sioux. Anyone who had much was expected to share with those who had little. When someone died, his family would hold a giveaway to distribute bison robes, horses, blankets, and furs to the other members of the tiyospaye. Today, many Sioux continue to practice giveaways. But now giveaways usually celebrate a happy occasion such as a birth, marriage, or graduation. The family hosting the giveaway hands out blankets, beadwork, quilts, clothing, and other items to those in attendance.*

provide them with rations in return. But the food was always late or insufficient, and the Dakota were slowly starving. They decided to mount a war party to push settlers off the lands they had given up. Dakota warriors rode through south-central Minnesota, killing more than 500 settlers and 70 U.S. soldiers. Afterward, more than 300 Dakota warriors were sentenced to death. President Abraham Lincoln **COMMUTED** the sentences of most, but 38 Dakota were hanged in Mankato, Minnesota, in what remains America's largest mass execution. The rest of the Dakota population was removed to reservations in Dakota Territory and Nebraska.

Farther west, the Lakota faced their own problems. Settlers eager to reach gold fields in Montana had established a trail through the heart of hunting grounds that had been promised to the Lakota by treaty. The army set up a series of forts along the route, which they named the Bozeman Trail. The Sioux called it the Thieves' Road, and they retaliated. Under the guidance of Oglala chief **RED CLOUD**, they set the Americans' horses and mules free. They attacked travelers on the trail and ambushed soldiers guarding the forts.

Then, in December 1866, Red Cloud assigned a young warrior

IN THE MID-1860S, SITTING BULL (ABOVE) BEGAN ATTACKING AMERICANS WHO TRIED TO TAKE OVER THE BLACK HILLS (RIGHT).

named **CRAZY HORSE** to draw the American soldiers at Fort Phil Kearny into an ambush. U.S. troops under Captain William Fetterman fell for the trick and pursued Crazy Horse. All 80 of the soldiers under Fetterman's command were killed in what became known as the Fetterman Fight.

After the Fetterman Fight, the U.S. agreed to give up its forts along the Bozeman Trail by signing a second Treaty of Fort Laramie (1868). In return, the Sioux were required to move onto the newly created Great Sioux Reservation, which encompassed all of South Dakota west of the Missouri River. The new treaty guaranteed that no one but the Indians would "ever be permitted to pass over, settle upon, or reside in" that land.

The promise wasn't kept for long. In 1874, the U.S. government sent Lieutenant Colonel **GEORGE ARMSTRONG CUSTER** to lead a scouting mission into the Black Hills, which were part of the Great Sioux Reservation. Custer's report that the hills were full of gold "from the grass roots down" triggered a swarm of gold miners to descend onto the Sioux's sacred land. When the Sioux complained, the government offered to purchase the land from them. But the Sioux weren't interested in selling. "One does not sell the earth upon which the people walk," Crazy Horse said of the government's offer. Hunkpapa Sioux chief **SITTING BULL** warned, "We want no white men here. The Black Hills belong to me. If the whites try to take them, I will fight." The government ignored his warning.

Although the 1868 Treaty of Fort Laramie had created the Great Sioux Reservation, many Sioux rejected the treaty and continued to live or hunt in lands farther west. But in late 1875, the government ordered that all Sioux make their way to the reservations by January 31, 1876. In June of that year, army units were sent to pursue the several thousand Sioux who had not complied. One unit was led by Custer, who split his men into three battalions to attack an Indian encampment near the Little Bighorn River in Montana Territory. Custer led one of the battalions himself. With about 200 men under his direct command, Custer launched an attack on the encampment, which may have numbered 1,800 to 2,000 allied Lakota, Cheyenne, and Arapaho warriors under the leadership of strong chiefs such as Crazy Horse and Sitting Bull. Within an hour, the now-infamous Battle of the Little Bighorn was over. Custer and his 200 men were dead.

The Lakota victory over Custer did not win them back their land. Instead, angered over what they termed a "massacre," the government threatened to withhold all rations until the Sioux signed over the Black Hills. In 1877, the Sioux were forced to give up their sacred mountains to the U.S. government.

A few Sioux bands, including those led by Crazy Horse and Sitting Bull, remained off the reservations, trying to eke out a living by hunting. But

AS THE SIOUX PREPARED FOR THE BATTLE OF THE LITTLE BIGHORN, SITTING BULL HAD A VISION OF CUSTER'S DEFEAT.

IN PROGRESS SINCE 1948, THE CRAZY HORSE MEMORIAL IS BEING CARVED FROM THUNDER-HEAD MOUNTAIN.

the bison that had once numbered 50 million or more had been whittled away to near-extinction by settlers. Faced with starvation, Crazy Horse, Sitting Bull, and the remaining free Sioux eventually surrendered.

Life on the reservation wasn't any easier, though, and many Sioux fell into despair. Around 1890, some found hope in a new religious movement known as the Ghost Dance. Indians performed the dance in the hopes that it would lead to peace and the disappearance of white men from their lands. The Ghost Dance made U.S. leaders nervous, and they banned it. Because Sitting Bull did not put a stop to the forbidden dance on his reservation, Sioux police were sent to arrest him. When Sitting Bull's followers tried to prevent the arrest, a fight broke out, and the famous chief was killed.

Alarmed by the violence, a group of Sioux led by Sitting Bull's half-brother Big Foot decided to seek safety on another reservation. But they were intercepted by U.S. soldiers at Wounded Knee Creek, South Dakota. While the soldiers were attempting to take away the Sioux's guns, a shot was fired, and a fight broke out. In the end, more than 200 Sioux men, women, and children were killed. A Sioux holy man named Black Elk later remembered the

WOUNDED KNEE, AGAIN *On February 27, 1973, 200 Indians staged an armed takeover of the town of Wounded Knee, where more than 200 Sioux had been killed in 1890. They demanded that the government change their tribal leadership, review all Indian treaties, and investigate U.S. treatment of Indians. The group was soon surrounded by government forces. The two sides exchanged gunfire, and a standoff lasted for 71 days. When the Indians surrendered on May 8, the town of Wounded Knee was in shambles. Two Indians had been killed, and one federal agent had been paralyzed.*

scene: "I can still see the butchered women and children lying heaped and scattered all along the crooked gulch.... And I can see that something else died there in the bloody mud.... A people's dream died there."

Conditions on the reservations did not improve after Wounded Knee. The Americans in charge of the reservations insisted that the Sioux give up their traditional way of life. "The government ... desires to teach you to become farmers, and to civilize you, and make you as white men," government agents had once told Sitting Bull. But farming went against the Sioux way of life, and the reservation land was ill-suited to it. The government was supposed to supply rations to the Sioux as well, but these were often inadequate or were stolen by corrupt Indian agents (people who were supposed to deal with the Indians on the government's behalf). As a result, many Sioux were near starving. Poor nutrition and inadequate housing led to the spread of diseases such as **TUBERCULOSIS** on many reservations. In addition, the Sioux were banned from practicing their traditional religion, and Sioux parents were required to send their children to boarding schools.

Conditions improved slightly with the signing of the Indian Reorganization Act in 1934. This act allowed the Sioux to govern themselves to some extent. It also removed the ban on traditional Indian practices. Even so, from the 1930s to the 1960s, many Sioux left the reservations to find jobs on nearby ranches or in large cities such as Minneapolis–St. Paul, Denver, and Los Angeles. In the 1960s and '70s, conditions on reservations began to improve, and some Sioux moved back.

Today, an estimated 160,000 Sioux live in the U.S. and Canada. About half live on reservations, mostly in South Dakota. For many Sioux, life on the reservations continues to be hard,

INHABITANTS OF THE PINE RIDGE RESERVATION WERE LIVING IN SOD-AND-LOG HOUSES IN THE EARLY 20TH CENTURY.

To preserve the
health of their
farms and people,
some activists
(right) have
tried to block
energy companies'
projects.

with high levels of poverty and unemployment. Healthcare on
many reservations continues to lag behind the rest of the coun-
try, and alcoholism rates are above the national average.

Many reservations have worked hard to create jobs and in-
come opportunities for their people, though. Some have opened
ranches and factories that employ a number of workers. On many
reservations, the biggest employers are casinos. In addition to
creating jobs, reservation casinos also distribute a portion of their
profits to the people living on the reservation.

As they work to create new opportunities for their people,
some reservations have also continued their fight with the U.S.
government. In 2014, the Oglala Sioux protested a proposed
expansion of the Keystone XL oil pipeline through its lands.
"Keystone XL is a death warrant for our people," said Oglala
Sioux tribal president Bryan Brewer. "The United States needs to
respect our treaty rights."

In addition to arguing over new treaty violations, the Sioux
continue to pursue the return of their sacred Black Hills. In 1980,
the Supreme Court offered the Sioux more than $100 million
as payment for the Black Hills, but the Sioux rejected the offer.
Although the money continues to collect interest and is today

Standing in the water could get me arrested.
TransCanada pollutes drinking water
and nothing happens.

⤛⤜ AT THE MOVIES ⤛⤜ *When most people think of the Indians of the past, they think of the Sioux. That's probably because for years, the Indians pictured in books, movies, and Wild West shows have been modeled after the Sioux. But these images are often inaccurate, with the Indians speaking the wrong language or wearing the wrong clothing. In recent years, attempts have been made to more accurately show the Sioux lifestyle through movies such as* Dances with Wolves *(1990) and* Bury My Heart at Wounded Knee *(2007).*

worth more than $1 billion, the Sioux insist that they will be satisfied only with the return of their land.

Even without their sacred land, though, many Sioux people have revived traditional practices and ceremonies. Schools on reservations and in areas with large Sioux populations teach the Dakota or Lakota languages and offer courses in Sioux history. Some Sioux continue to practice the annual Sun Dance ceremony, embark on vision quests, and consult medicine men. Sioux living on and off the reservations come together each summer for powwows featuring feasts, songs, and traditional dances. Non-Indians are invited to these ceremonies, too, to learn more about Sioux culture.

The revival of traditional practices has led many, such as **ANTHROPOLOGIST** Guy Gibbon, to conclude that the Sioux nation "is alive and healthier than it has been since the early 19th century." The life of the Sioux people has changed much over the past 1,000 years. From their early days in the northern woodlands to their glory years riding horses across the Great Plains to their struggles against encroaching settlers, every experience has reshaped the Sioux nation. Today, they are a vibrant, diverse people, sharing their culture with one another and the world.

ONEIDA ACTOR GRAHAM GREENE PLAYED THE LAKOTA CHARACTER KICKING BIRD IN *DANCES WITH WOLVES*.

*Many traditional Sioux stories were about Iktomi, a spider that
can transform into a man. Although the Sioux considered Iktomi
sacred, they also thought of him as a trickster who was "good
and bad at the same time." In this story, which was handed down
from generation to generation during the long winters on the
Plains, Iktomi's actions teach a lesson about bravery.*

One summer day when Iktomi was walking through
the high grasses of the Plains, he came upon a herd
of elk. He admired the elk's sleek coats and tall antlers. When he looked at his own reflection in a stream, he felt
small and ugly.

So Iktomi approached the chief elk. He asked the elk to
make him part of his tribe. The elk hesitated. He had heard
that Iktomi was a coward. But Iktomi promised he was a great
warrior who had counted coup and earned many eagle feathers. Iktomi assured the elk that his eyes, ears, and nose were
sharp to detect danger.

So the elk chief said Iktomi could join the tribe. But Iktomi
wasn't satisfied. He asked the elk to make him tall and powerful like the elk. So the elk chief did. Then Iktomi asked the elk
to give him a sleek, shiny elk coat. So the elk chief did. Then
Iktomi asked the elk to give him stately antlers. The elk chief
again did what was asked. Iktomi was proud of his new form.
He boasted that he was the strongest, bravest,
most handsome elk in the tribe.

One day, Iktomi was resting when a small twig fell on him. He thought he was hit by an arrow, and he jumped up and started to run, crying, "Enemies! Enemies!" The rest of the herd stampeded behind him. But the elk soon noticed that there were no enemies. They were annoyed with Iktomi for scaring so easily.

A few days later, Iktomi was again resting with the herd. An acorn fell on him. This time, he thought he was hit by a bullet. Again he cried out that enemies were in the camp. And again he led a stampede across the Plains. When the elk realized this had been another false alarm, they warned Iktomi to be braver.

A few more days went by. As Iktomi was walking through the grass to graze, he was scratched by thorns. "Enemies!" he yelled. "Wolves are biting me!" This time, though, the elk didn't stampede. They told Iktomi there were no wolves in the area. The chief accused Iktomi of being a coward.

In the middle of the night, Iktomi woke up to the sound of something rustling in the bushes. He sent out the alarm that hundreds of enemies were attacking. But the elk looked in the bushes and found a rabbit.

By now, the elk were tired of Iktomi's fear. So the next night, they left Iktomi while he slept. When he woke up, he was alone. And in place of his strong elk form, he was once again a small spider-man. But no one felt bad for him, since it was his own fault for crying wolf so many times.

ALTAR
a table or raised structure used in the performance of religious ceremonies

ANTHROPOLOGIST
someone who studies the physical traits, cultures, and relationships of different peoples

CHOLERA
a disease that causes nausea, vomiting, diarrhea, and severe dehydration

COMMUTED
substituted a less severe punishment in place of the original sentence

CRAZY HORSE
(c. 1842–77) Oglala Sioux chief who helped lead Sioux forces against Custer at the Battle of the Little Bighorn; afterward, he escaped but surrendered in 1877 and was killed a few months later during an arrest attempt

DIALECT
a form of a language that uses specific pronunciations, grammar, or vocabularies that differ from other forms of the language; speakers of different dialects of the same language can usually understand each other

FASTED
went without eating, often as part of a religious ritual

GEORGE ARMSTRONG CUSTER
(1839–76) a U.S. Army officer in the Civil War who later led the U.S. 7th Cavalry in the attack at the Little Bighorn, in which he and all 200 men in his command were killed

MEDICINE MAN
a spiritual leader often believed to have healing and other powers

NOMADIC
moving from place to place rather than living in a permanent home

OREGON TRAIL
a route leading across the Great Plains to the northwestern U.S.; thousands of settlers followed this trail between the 1840s and 1870s

PICTOGRAPH
a form of writing in which a picture or symbol stands for an idea

RED CLOUD
(1822–1909) Oglala Sioux chief who led resistance efforts against the development of white roads through Sioux territory; he moved to a reservation in 1868 but traveled frequently to Washington, D.C., to criticize the government's Indian policy

SINEW
a tendon, or cord, that connects muscle to bone

SITTING BULL
(c. 1831–90) Hunkpapa Sioux chief who led Sioux forces at the Battle of the Little Bighorn and afterward escaped into Canada before surrendering in 1881; he was killed by Sioux police in 1890 during an arrest attempt

TRAVOIS
a vehicle made of two poles crossed into a V-shape at one end, with a bison hide hung between them to serve as a platform; the travois was hitched to a dog or horse, with the ends dragging on the ground

TUBERCULOSIS
a contagious disease that causes fever, cough, and difficulty breathing

Brown, Dee. *Bury My Heart at Wounded Knee: An Indian History of the American West*. New York: Sterling, 2009.

Cassidy, James, ed. *Through Indian Eyes: The Untold Story of Native American Peoples*. Pleasantville, N.Y.: Reader's Digest, 1995.

Erdoes, Richard. *Native Americans: The Sioux*. New York: Sterling, 1982.

Gibbon, Guy. *The Sioux: The Dakota and Lakota Nations*. Malden, Mass.: Blackwell, 2003.

Hyman, Colette A. *Dakota Women's Work: Creativity, Culture & Exile*. St. Paul: Minnesota Historical Society, 2012.

Mails, Thomas E. *The Mystic Warriors of the Plains*. New York: Mallard Press, 1991.

Page, Jake. *In the Hands of the Great Spirit: The 20,000-Year History of American Indians*. New York: Free Press, 2003.

Palmer, Jessica Dawn. *The Dakota Peoples: A History of the Dakota, Lakota, and Nakota through 1863*. Jefferson, N.C.: McFarland, 2008.

Levine, Michelle. *The Sioux*. Minneapolis: Lerner, 2007.

Remington, Gwen. *The Sioux*. San Diego: Lucent, 2000.

AKTA LAKOTA MUSEUM & CULTURAL CENTER
http://aktalakota.stjo.org
Find out more about Lakota culture, language, and beliefs and read a sampling of traditional Lakota stories.

TRACKING THE BUFFALO:
STORIES FROM A BUFFALO HIDE PAINTING
http://americanhistory.si.edu/buffalo/
Learn more about the importance of the bison to the Sioux and other Plains Indians. See if you can figure out what the pictures on a painted hide mean.

NOTE: EVERY EFFORT HAS BEEN MADE TO ENSURE THAT THE WEBSITES LISTED ABOVE ARE SUITABLE FOR CHILDREN, THAT THEY HAVE EDUCATIONAL VALUE, AND THAT THEY CONTAIN NO INAPPROPRIATE MATERIAL. HOWEVER, BECAUSE OF THE NATURE OF THE INTERNET, IT IS IMPOSSIBLE TO GUARANTEE THAT THESE SITES WILL REMAIN ACTIVE INDEFINITELY OR THAT THEIR CONTENTS WILL NOT BE ALTERED.